ANTIQUE
QUILTING DESIGNS
Roberta Benvin

American Quilter's Society

P. O. Box 3290 • Paducah, KY 42002-3290
www.AQSquilt.com

Located in Paducah, Kentucky, the American Quilter's Society (AQS) is dedicated to promoting the accomplishments of today's quilters. Through its publications and events, AQS strives to honor today's quiltmakers and their work and to inspire future creativity and innovation in quiltmaking.

EDITOR: SHELLEY HAWKINS
TECHNICAL EDITOR: HELEN SQUIRE
GRAPHIC DESIGN: LYNDA SMITH
COVER DESIGN: MICHAEL BUCKINGHAM
PHOTOGRAPHY: HAYMAN STUDIO

Library of Congress Cataloging-in-Publication Data
Roberta Benvin.
  Antique Quilting Designs / by Roberta Benvin.
    p. cm.
  ISBN 1-57432-769-0
  1. . 2. Quilting--Patterns. 3. . I.
Roberta Benvin. II. Title.
  TT835 .S78 20012
    746.46'041--dc21

                          200100

Additional copies of this book may be ordered from the American Quilter's Society, PO Box 3290,
Paducah, KY 42002-3290, or online at www.AQSquilt.com.

Dedication

To my daughter, Kelly,
who thinks the main reason I love antique
quilts is because I managed to find
something older than myself.

To my daughter, Erin,
who cannot understand how a person
can have such an all-consuming passion
for quilts (after all, they're not horses).

To my son, Erik,
whose talent for art I would give
anything to possess.

Acknowledgments

My sincerest thanks

…To my "mother" Linda Smith,
my "sister" Debbie Goldman,
and my "bud" Joan Hamme,
whose steadfast friendship and
support have been such a blessing.

To Eleanor Eckman, who offered to quilt
whatever I needed for this publication and
for her magnificent hand quilting on my wallhanging.

To the York County Quilt Documentation Project Committee
for permission to access its research material.

To every one of the generous quilt owners who made this book possible, and to the quiltmakers
of the past who have reminded me that to quilt is to express the joy of creativity in one's soul.

Contents

Preface

In researching quilts for this book, a collection that was obviously influenced by the Pennsylvania German folk art style was revealed. For the sake of continuity, I decided to focus on this particular genre. It was a pleasant surprise to discover this fascinating style of quilting designs of which I was totally unaware. I believe there is a need to record and preserve this facet of our quilting heritage.

Throughout the text, the terms "Pennsylvania German" and "Pennsylvania Dutch" are used interchangeably. However, the Pennsylvania Germans (Dutch) to whom I refer are not the "plain people" (Amish and Mennonites), but the "church people" (also known as fancy or gaudy Dutch) who were Lutherans and Reformed.

Although my tracings of the quilting designs are refined to a certain degree, they are not drawn, nor do I feel they should be, with the accuracy such as that of a laser-cut stencil. The majority of these designs were probably hand-drafted and some of the flavor and character of folk art should be maintained. All of the quilting patterns are full size, just as they appear on their respective quilts.

Unfortunately, none of the quilts in this book have been inscribed with the name of the maker or the date it was made. However, the owners have made every effort to determine the origin of the quilts. Dating was based on the fabric as well as other clues that were taken into consideration.

Introduction

From my start in quilting, I have had an intense interest in antique quilts. I became involved in the restoration of antique quilts, treasuring the time they were in my possession. Then, the most glorious experience of all presented itself – my involvement in the quilt documentation project of York County, Pennsylvania.[1] Unlike many regions in Pennsylvania that are characterized by quilts of recurrent designs, fabrics, or techniques, York County had a bit of everything. What caught my attention was the seemingly higher-than-average number of quilts containing an assortment of quilting designs, or "quilting samplers," as referred by Barbara Brackman.[2]

For the past several years, I have made antique reproduction quilts, taking advantage of the ever-increasing number of reproduction lines available from fabric manufacturers. Nearing completion of a particular quilt top, I realized that no consideration had been given to how it should be quilted. It would be wonderful if I could put authentic early nineteenth-century designs on the reproduction quilt. The thought of those quilting samplers came to mind immediately as a source for the designs.

It occurred to me there might be other quiltmakers seeking a readily available collection of early quilting patterns. From that moment, my quest began to trace as many of these designs as possible. With the characteristic friendliness and generosity of York Countians, the owners allowed me complete access to their quilts, for which I shall be forever grateful.

Initially, the concept of compiling a book of early quilting designs seemed relatively uncomplicated: trace the designs, refine the rough drawings, and add a modicum of text to describe the provenance of each quilt. After working on just a few blocks from the first quilt, the similarity of the quilting designs to common motifs of early Pennsylvania German folk art was intriguing. This occurred again with the second quilt and, particularly, the third. I wondered if the designs had been chosen purposefully for these quilts, which by their very nature seemed to indicate they were wedding spreads. On the other hand, the designs may have been selected solely on the basis of their attractiveness and availability.

In her book, *Spoken Without a Word*, Elly Sienkiewicz proposed the concept that the "good ladies of Baltimore" engaged in the use of symbolic imagery when selecting the individual elements in their elaborate and exquisitely crafted appliqué album blocks.[3] Perhaps it is conceivable that this fascination with symbolism extended beyond the city limits of Baltimore, into the pastoral regions of southeastern Pennsylvania. It was

[1]The York County Quilt Documentation Committee, *QUILTS, The Fabric of Friendship,* Schiffer Publishing Ltd., Atglen, Pennsylvania.
[2]Barbara Brackman, *Clues in the Calico: A Guide to Identifying and Dating Antique Quilts,* EPM Publications, Inc., 1989, p. 112.
[3]Elly Sienkiewicz, *Spoken Without a Word,* published by the author, 1983, p. 19.

Introduction

approximately the same period in time – the 1840s and 1850s. Though the women of these two locales had little in common in terms of wealth and sophistication, they shared traditions rooted in Christianity. The origin of many of these motifs can be traced to Europe and even ancient Greece.

It appeared obvious, at least from my perspective as a quilter, that the hearts and interlocking circles were an indication of a quilt intended to celebrate a marriage. It was especially obvious as these and other designs kept appearing on one quilt after another.

Thoroughly intrigued, I read every source of information available on Pennsylvania German folk art and its possible symbolism. I pored over articles and books by such noted Pennsylvania German historians as Alfred Shoemaker, John Joseph Stoudt, Frances Lichten, and many, many more. My only determination was that no one was willing to say with any certainty that these motifs displayed indisputable symbolism. Virtually without exception, the historians indicated that the common and repetitive usage of these motifs more than likely was a "form of communicative expression" understood by the culture of that time.[4]

It is puzzling that none of the articles or books indicated conclusively whether or not these folk art designs defined specific symbolism. According to the historians, public awareness of Pennsylvania German folk art did not occur until the early years of the twentieth century. That was when automobile travel opened up the somewhat isolated areas of eastern Pennsylvania and books such as Wallace

Nutting's *Pennsylvania the Beautiful* attached the name "hex marks" to the decorative barn signs in that part of the state.

This sudden interest and stirring of the public's imagination demanded more information. Until this time, "it had not been common knowledge that these same designs had appeared at an earlier period on practically every object that was ever decorated in the Pennsylvania Dutch country – on dower chests, sgraffito plates, birth and baptismal certificates, hand-illuminated book plates, tool boxes on Conestoga wagons, the keystone arches of churches, even on tombstones."[5] By this time, very few inhabitants of the area remembered any exact meanings for the motifs, only an oral history unsubstantiated by written documentation.

Several of the designs that occurred and reoccurred on the majority of the quilts I examined apparently have a consensus of opinion as to their "silent" message. My insights are shared in this book and you are invited to draw your own conclusions.

As a quilter myself, I find it highly likely that my quiltmaking predecessors chose designs that conveyed a deeper sentiment than what was immediately obvious. In the words of John Joseph Stoudt, "all essential art is symbolic because it seeks to bridge two worlds with signs and devices that express deep, authentic reality."[6]

I hope you enjoy using these designs on your quilts. Feel free to invoke upon them any unspoken sentiments. Or you may want to use them, as the Pennsylvania Dutch might have, *chust for nice!*

---

[4]*Arts of the Pennsylvania Germans,* A Winterthur Book selected by the Pennsylvania German Society as Vol. 17 in its series by W.W. Norton & Co., 1983, p. IX.

[5]Alfred L. Shoemaker, editor, *The Pennsylvania Barn*, Pennsylvania Dutch Folklore Center, Inc., 1955, pp. 60–61.

[6]John Joseph Stoudt, *Pennsylvania German Folk Art – An Interpretation,* Pennsylvania German Folklore Society, Vol. 28, 1966.

PAST AND PRESENT DUTCH
52" x 52"
This quilt is a contemporary version of the PIECED DOUBLE NINE-PATCH QUILT.
Pieced and appliquéd by the author and quilted by Eleanor Eckman.

The border fabric, which positively shouted Pennsylvania Dutch to me, dictated the color scheme for the Double Nine-Patch blocks. Quilting patterns were selected from the original quilt to fill the alternate plain squares, thereby, combining a bit of the old and new in this piece.

PIECED DOUBLE NINE-PATCH QUILT, circa 1846

Attributed to Julia Ann Howlett Scarborough, Harford County, Maryland. Collection of Sara Wiley Robinson.

Once-elegant fabrics, no larger than ¾", make up the pieced squares in this Double Nine-Patch quilt. The alternate plain blocks are filled with a wonderful array of quilting patterns. There is a delicacy to the quilting designs, making them perfectly suited to the relatively small 7" blocks. None of the designs are identical; however, the wreaths are repeated with different motifs in the center.

A scalloped border appears to have been constructed by cutting apart a curved print and applying half along each edge of the muslin border. In addition to the maker's obvious artistic talents, she was a superlative quilter, with the stitches on the surface of the quilt ranging between 12–14 per inch.

It seems most likely that this remarkable quilt was made by or for Julia Ann Howlett Scarborough. Julia Ann was born in Harford County, Maryland, which is close to the Pennsylvania-Maryland border. She was a Quaker of English descent, but the quilting designs reflect a distinctive Pennsylvania German influence that was so much a part of that region. It is conceivable that the quilt was made circa 1846, when Julia Ann was married.

Page 12

Page 15

Page 13

Page 16

Page 14

Page 17

The tulip, which is the most recognizable motif used in Pennsylvania Dutch folk art, probably is an adaptation of the lily in Biblical reference. The word tulip is a corruption of the Turkish word meaning lily. One theory is that the tulip may be a symbol of fertility.[1] However, the most widely held opinion is that the tulip was used with such frequency simply because it was one of the easiest flower designs to draw.

Almost all Pennsylvania Dutch folk art has evolved from the religious beliefs of that culture. It is thought that tulips in a cluster of three may be a symbol of the Trinity.

[1]Fredric Klees, *The Pennsylvania Dutch*, p. 372.

Tombstone from Muddy Creek Lutheran and Reformed Church, founded 1732; East Cocalico Township, Lancaster County, PA.

Page 19

Page 22

Page 20

Page 23

Page 21

Page 24

The pineapple is a well-known symbol of hospitality.

Page 26

Page 28

Page 27

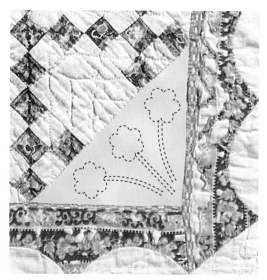

Page 28

Pages 29–31

border corner square

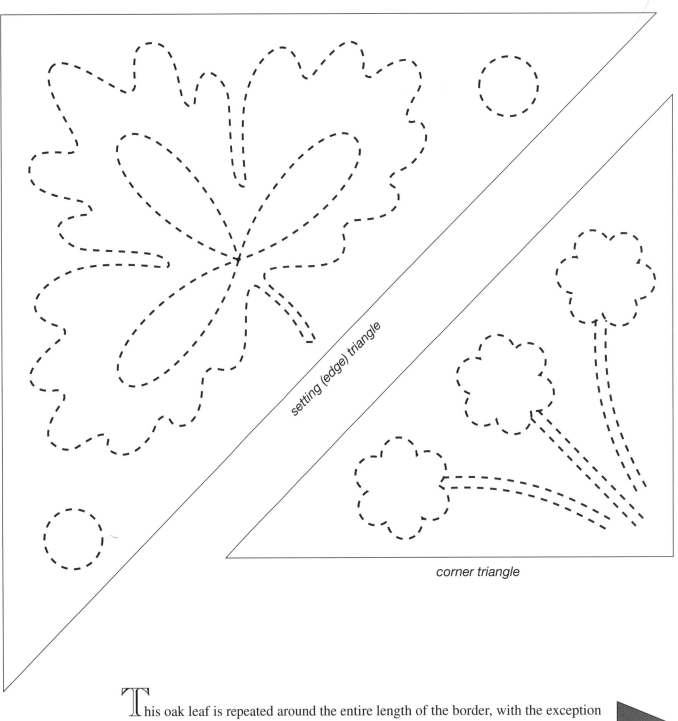

setting (edge) triangle

corner triangle

This oak leaf is repeated around the entire length of the border, with the exception of the corner squares. A simple, small botanical motif accompanies each larger leaf. The motifs included here may be repeated or you may create some of your own.

In Pennsylvania Dutch symbolism, the oak leaf represents strength, and as such, seems a fitting choice for the edge of a quilt.

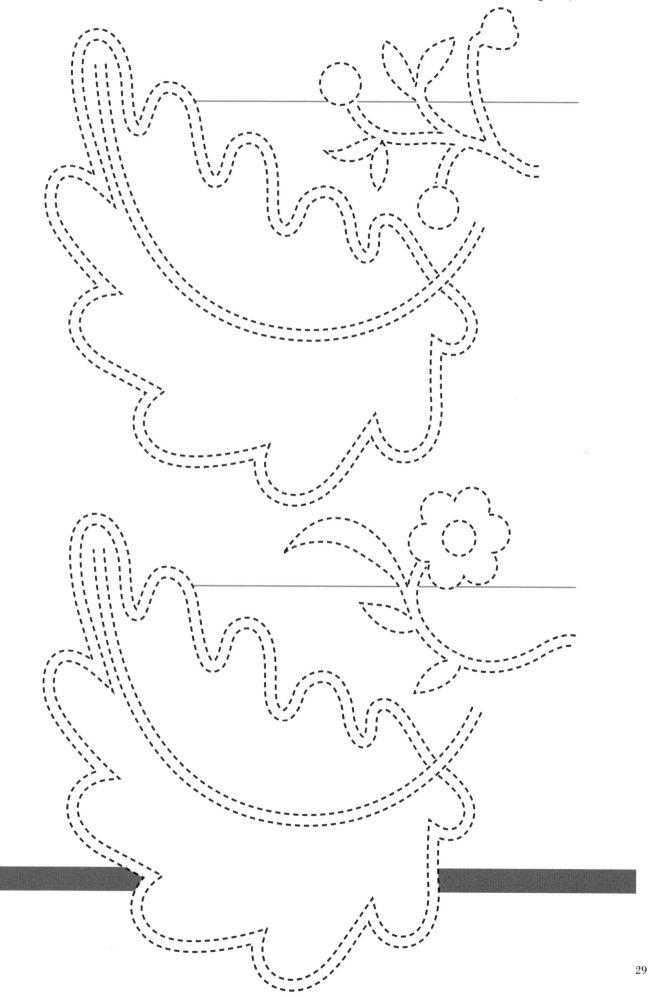

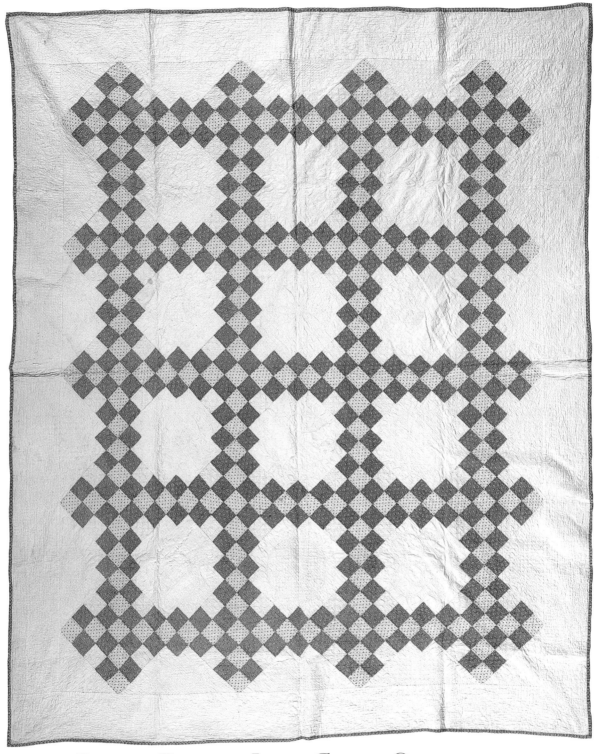

PIECED DOUBLE IRISH CHAIN QUILT, circa 1835
Attributed to Christina Flinchbaugh Tyson,
Felton, York County, Pennsylvania. Collection of L. Elizabeth Weimer and Virginia E. Brenner.

The owner believes her great-great-grandmother, Christina Flinchbaugh Tyson (b. 1808, d. 1886), probably made the quilt. Members of the Tyson family were well-known in the southern York County, Pennsylvania, area as skilled weavers and quilters. In fact, during the last quarter of the nineteenth century and through the 1920s, two spinster sisters, Amanda and Ellie Tyson, made their living by quilting for others. The Turkey red and chrome yellow prints date the quilt to the 1830s, which coincides with Christina's marriage to Benjamin Tyson in 1836. Quilting stitches average 10–12 stitches to the inch on the top of the quilt.

From a distance, there does not appear to be anything extraordinary about the PIECED DOUBLE IRISH CHAIN QUILT (page 32). However, a closer examination reveals an incredible variety of quilting designs in the alternate blocks. The motifs that include hearts, interlocking circles, and symbols of good luck are an indication that this most likely was a wedding quilt.

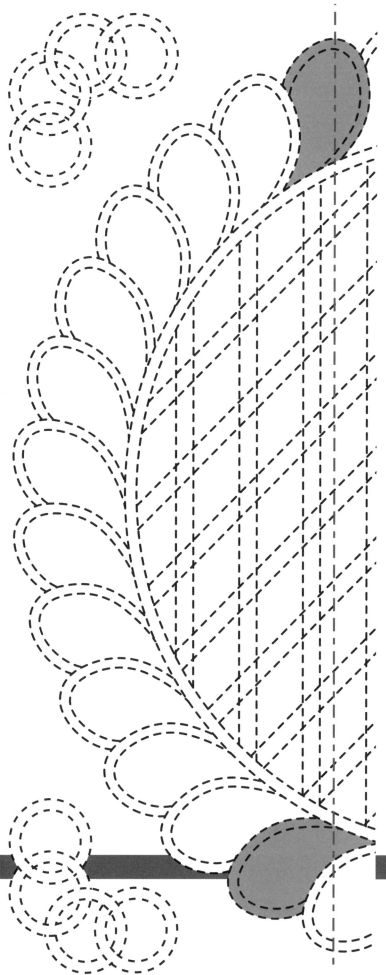

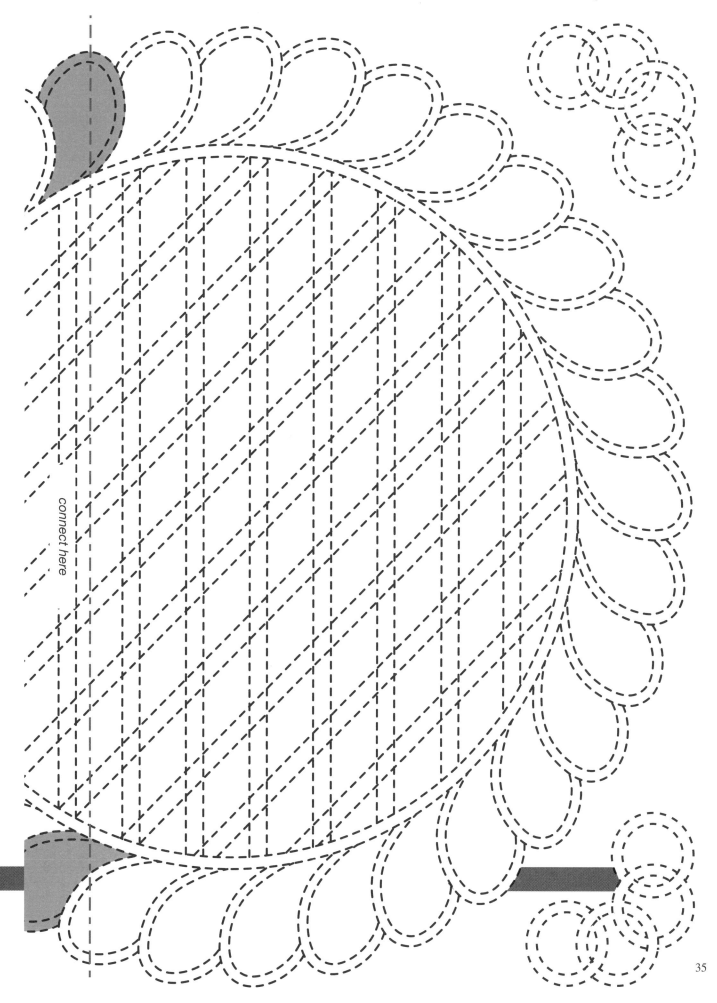

connect here

*rotate
feather
border*

*rotate scallop borders and
connect for full pattern*

connect here

connect here

Scallops, found in so many of these wreaths, are believed to invoke smooth sailing through life, which is a fitting sentiment for a bride of any century.

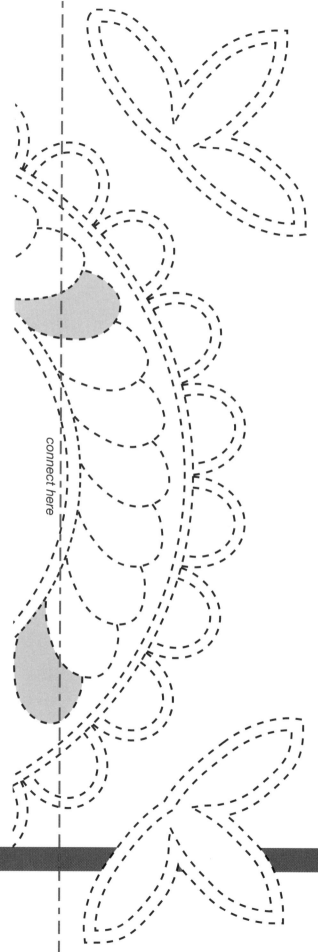

connect here

Small motifs filling the corners of the block are seen frequently in Pennsylvania Dutch artwork, as evident on this illuminated bookplate.

Courtesy of Dover Publications. AUTHENTIC PENNSYLVANIA DUTCH DESIGNS *by Frances Lichten.*

connect here

The six-pointed rosette is known as a *gluckstern*, or lucky star. In Europe, it has always been a symbol of good luck.

placement diagrams

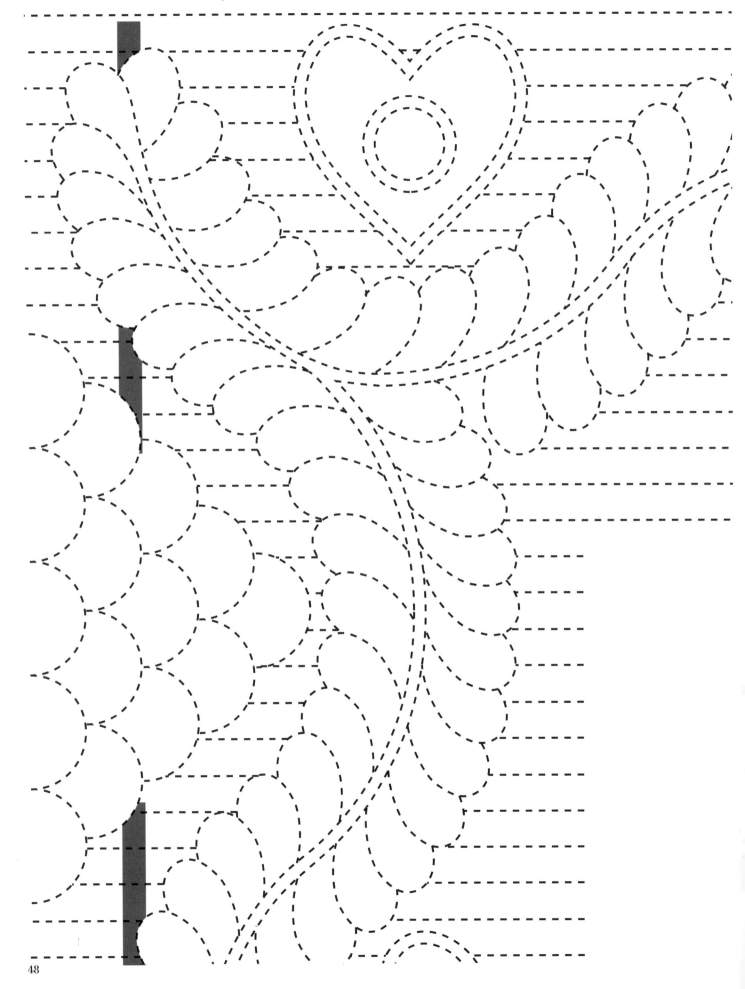

This section of the border may be used as often as needed to achieve the desired length for your quilt. Notice the curves on one side of the feather cable are going in the opposite direction from those on the other side.

The various designs in the "hills and valleys" echo those found in the blocks and seem to have been placed randomly. Allow yourself the same spontaneity when making your choice of these designs.

Antique Quilting Designs – *Roberta Benvin*

Pieced Double Irish Chain Quilt, circa 1835

This is a beautifully executed corner – the way one is taught that all four corners should be drafted. However, the "make-do" handling of corners on most antique quilts (such as the corner treatment on page 48) still looks wonderful.

Pieced Double Irish Chain Quilt, circa 1840

Attributed to Rebecca Wiley Marsteller,
New Park, York County, Pennsylvania. Collection of Carol Lowe Morris.

From both near and far, this Double Irish Chain quilt is nothing less than wonderful. Despite its age, it remains in pristine condition. The pieced squares are a combination of a single red calico and a vibrant yellow fabric with small botanical figure. The border is chintz with floral bouquets. A solid red square is set on point in each of the four corners. The quilting stitches were counted at nine to ten per inch. Since the fabrics date the quilt to the 1840s, it seems most likely that it was made by Rebecca Wiley Marsteller, about whom only her birth

in 1807 is known. She married Henry Marsteller probably in the year 1829, since their first of three children was born in 1830. Henry Marsteller's ancestors came to Pennsylvania from Germany in 1729.

The quilt was passed down through the daughter of each generation until it came into the possession of Rebecca's great-great-granddaughters, Mary and Nellie Lowe. They presented it to its current owner who is also a great-great-granddaughter.

connect here

connect here

Raindrops, believed to be a symbol of fertility, are commonly seen in Pennsylvania Dutch folk art. They were prevalent on the barn signs that decorated eastern Pennsylvania barns in the mid-1800s.

*rotate to connect
full pattern*

*rotate to connect
full pattern*

rotate to connect
full pattern

*rotate to connect
full pattern*

rotate to connect
full pattern

connect here

This tombstone from a cemetery in Lancaster County, Pennsylvania, displays several designs often seen in quilting motifs, such as scallops, prairie points, fans, a heart, and the eight-point star.

Courtesy of the Collection of York County Heritage Trust.

The three-lobed leaves that show up frequently in several of the quilts in this book also appear on the bottom of this *Taufschein* (baptismal certificate). Also notable are the "fat" hearts that are so abundant on this quilt.

One quarter shown,
rotate to connect full pattern

*rotate to connect
full pattern*

*rotate to connect
full pattern*

Appliquéd Princess Feather/Rose Wreath Quilt, circa 1850
Attributed to Sallie Scott, southern York County, Pennsylvania.
Collection of Mr. and Mrs. George N. Bair.

It was delightful to find that quilting samplers were not confined solely to pieced quilts. In this beautiful 1850s appliqué quilt, a Princess Feather-style plume dominates the center, surrounded by wreaths of roses, and framed with a tulip vine border. The quilting in the borders echoes the appliqué in the vine.

A single green print is used in all of the wreaths, but at least five different Turkey red prints make up the flowers. Although both traditional and Pennsylvania German folk patterns are included,

the leaves give the appearance of having been picked from the tree and their outlines traced directly onto the quilt top.

The maker is thought to have been Sallie Scott, wife of John Scott, both of Scots-Irish heritage. Unfortunately, little else, including their wedding date, is known. However, it is known that they had a daughter named Sally (possibly a nickname for Sarah) Leeper Scott Barnett. It is through her descendants that the quilt has come into the possession of its present owners.

Along with the designs featured in the centers of the wreaths, additional quilting motifs fill the spaces between the appliqués. The motifs are quilted with at least 10 stitches to the inch.

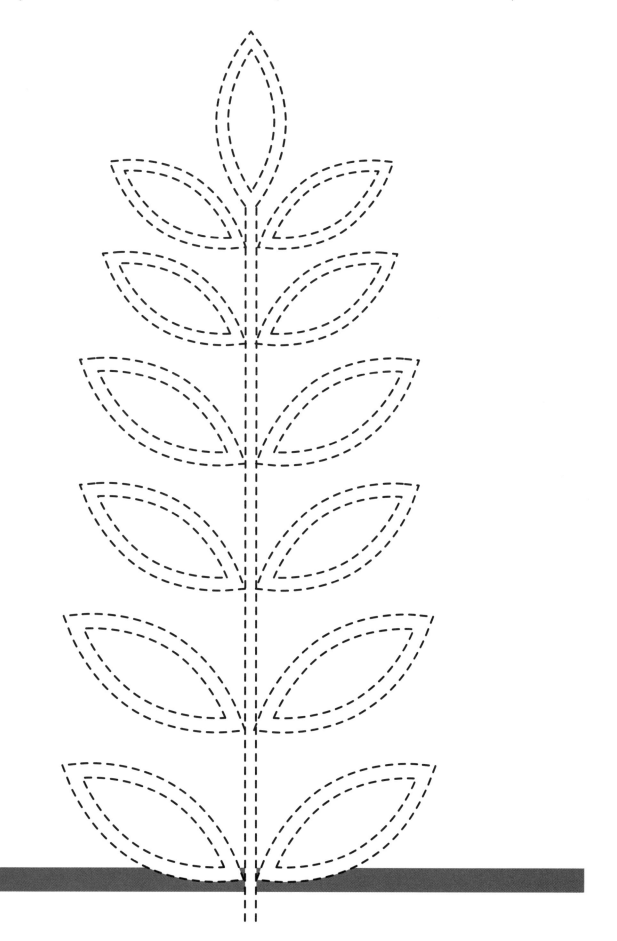

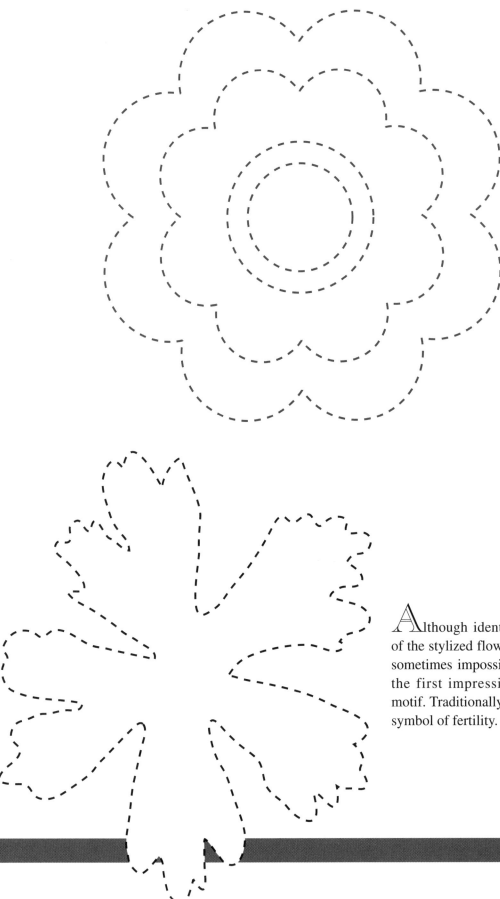

Although identification of many of the stylized flowers is difficult and sometimes impossible, a carnation is the first impression given by this motif. Traditionally, the carnation is a symbol of fertility.

A feature typical in each of these early quilts, very few spaces were left unstitched. Not only did quilting fill the inner portion of the wreaths, the areas between the wreaths were enhanced with similar and additional quilting designs. The motifs were repeated over and over again.

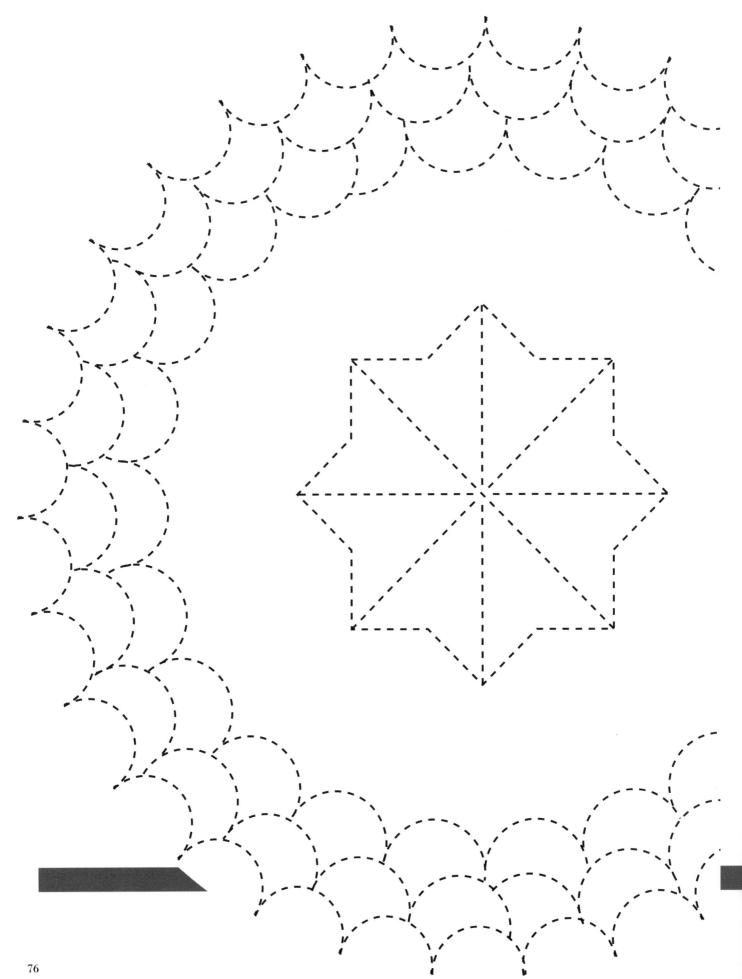

seam line

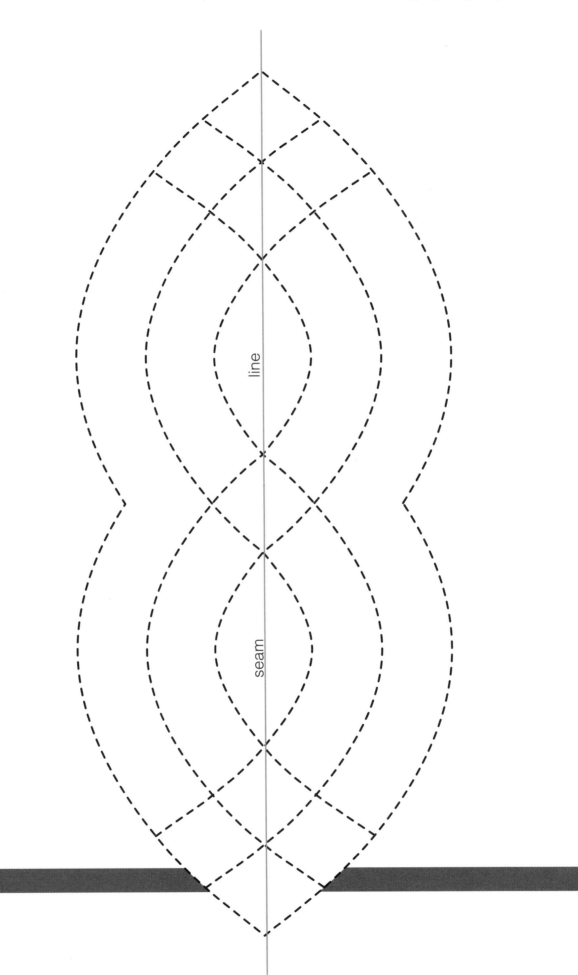

line

seam

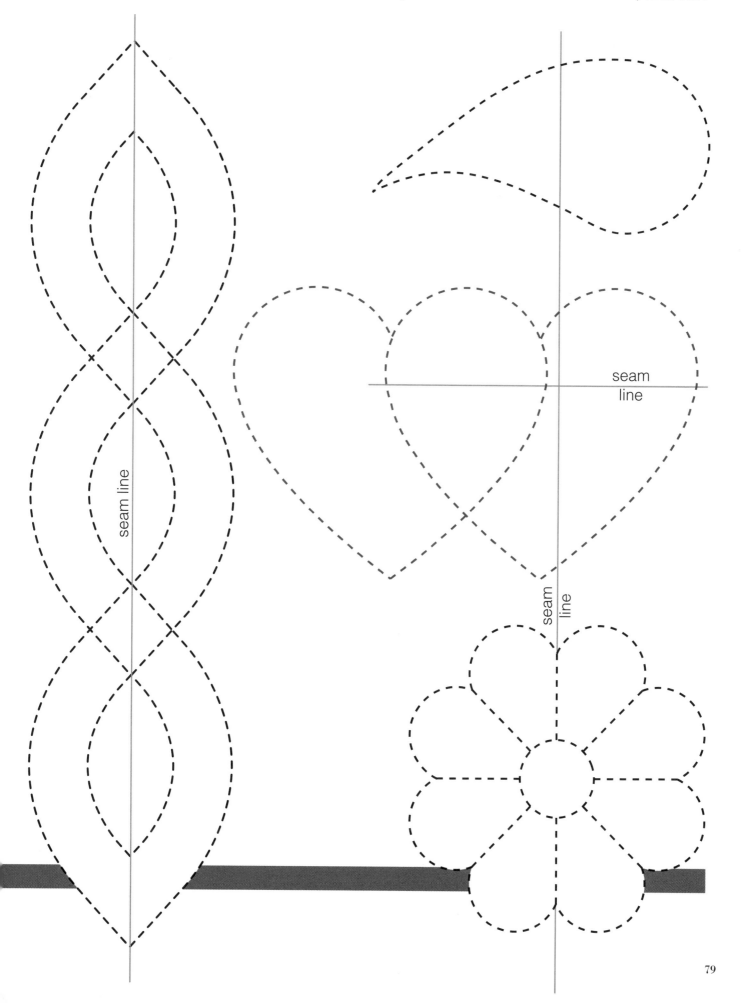

seam line

seam line

seam line

APPLIQUÉD QUILT, circa 1850
Attributed to Mary Smith Maughlin, Airville, York County, Pennsylvania.
Collection of Beth Grove Wittenbrader.

Mary Smith Maughlin, maker of this quilt, was also the maker of the PIECED DOUBLE IRISH CHAIN QUILT on page 94. Many of the quilting designs on this quilt appear on the Irish Chain quilt as well. The repeated designs include the clamshell and teacup patterns, the 6" feathered wreath, as well as other circular designs that have been reduced in size to fit the spaces between the appliqué. This particular appliqué pattern was possibly the maker's original design since its likeness was not found in any resource book. Stitches on this quilt average 10 to the inch.

The use of red and green color combinations in fabrics was certainly popular during the 1850s, as evident in this quilt.

The areas between the appliqué were filled with a combination of Pennsylvania Dutch-looking circular patterns and more traditional-looking elongated designs, such as the feathered cable, a delicate vine, and a repeat of the clamshell and teacup motifs.

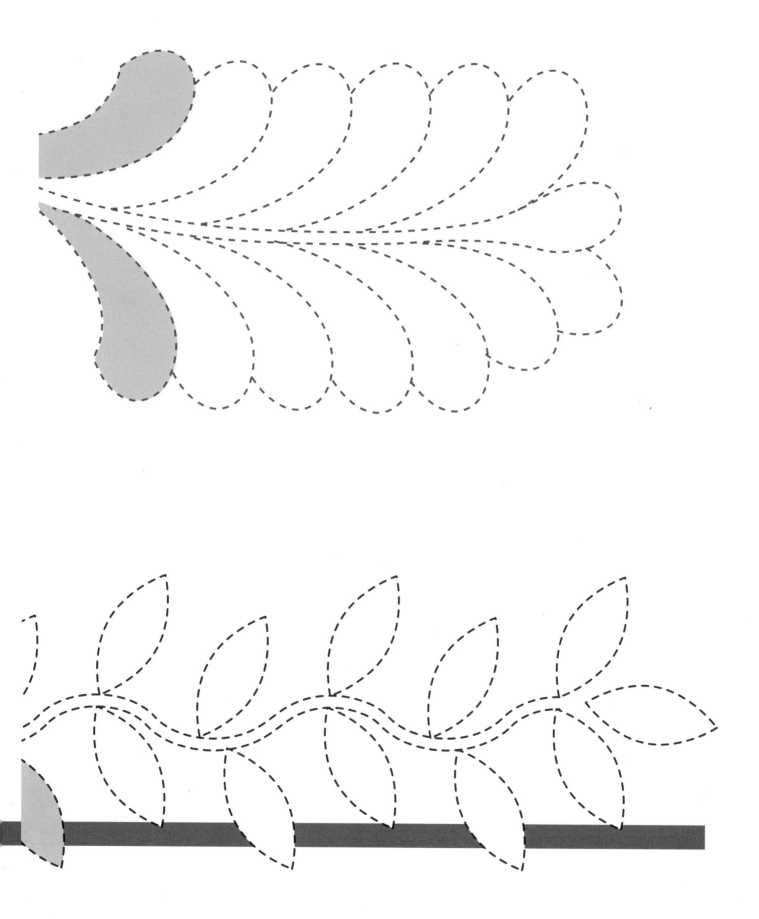

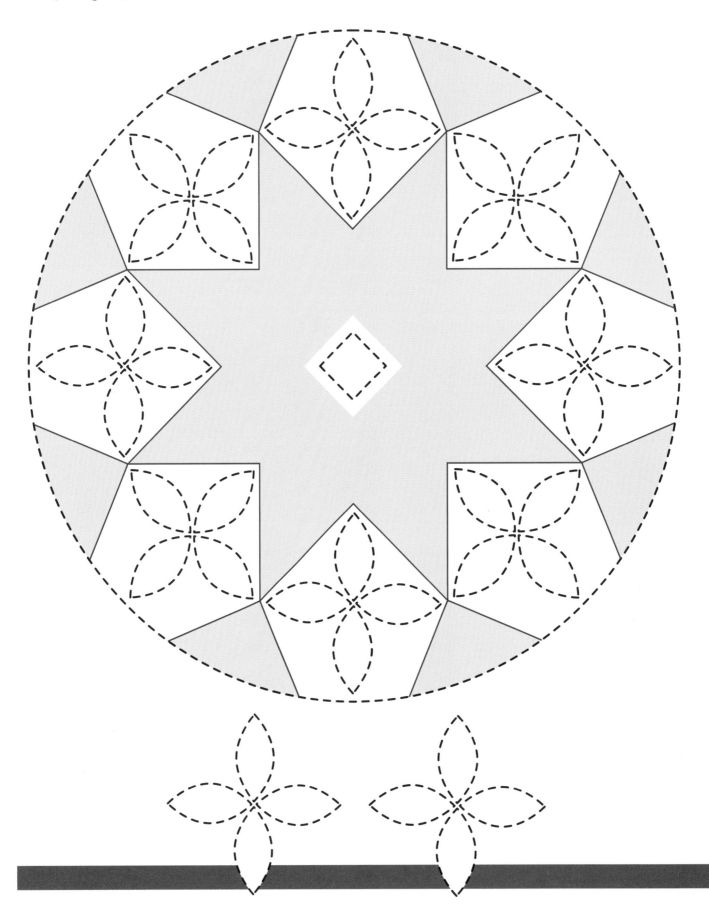

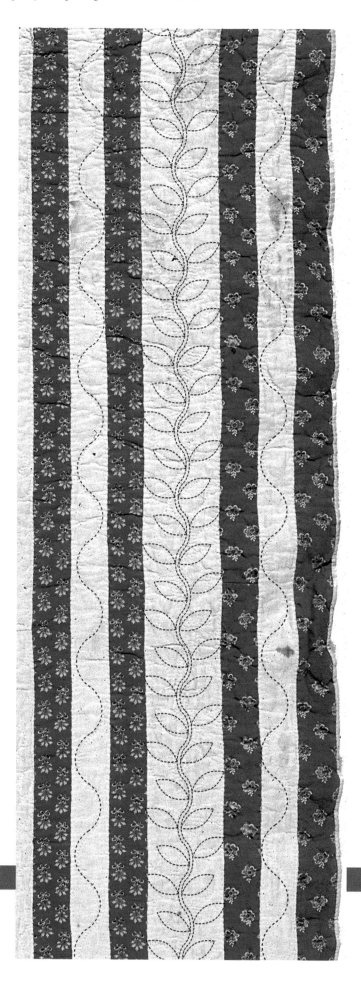

A total of seven narrow bands makes up the border section, culminating in beautifully appliquéd corner squares.

Appliquéd Oak Leaf and Reel Quilt, circa 1850

Attributed to Margaret Alexander Wiley Crawford, Peach Bottom Township, York County, Pennsylvania.
Collection of Nancy and Anne Smith.

Another appliqué quilt, this one featuring a beautiful Oak Leaf and Reel in a relatively large 16" x 17" block. The appliqués are cut from a red fabric that has a blue, white, and either a brown or black print. Apparently, the latter contained an iron mordant dye that oxidized and disintegrated, leaving a "swiss cheese" effect on the red material. Regardless, the overall impact of the quilt is stunning, and the floral chintz border is in splendid condition.

This quilt was a gift from Margaretta Wiley Wallace, the maker's granddaughter, to her lifelong best friend, Alice Anna McLaughlin Lee. Alice's granddaughters now treasure it.

Tulip designs were stitched in the spaces between the first and second rows.

Known by such names as swastika, four-leaved clover, whirling swastika, spinning whorl, and pinwheel, this motif has very ancient origins. It is used repeatedly in Pennsylvania Dutch folk art and is almost as familiar as the ubiquitous tulip. The name I prefer for the symbol, probably because it sounds so Dutch, is *fylfot*, a Teutonic compound meaning "many footed." From the many sources researched, the consensus seems to be that this is a symbol of good luck. Perhaps this explains the frequency with which it appears on these quilts that, quite possibly, were made in celebration of marriages. The *fylfot* filled each of the areas between the second and third rows of appliqué.

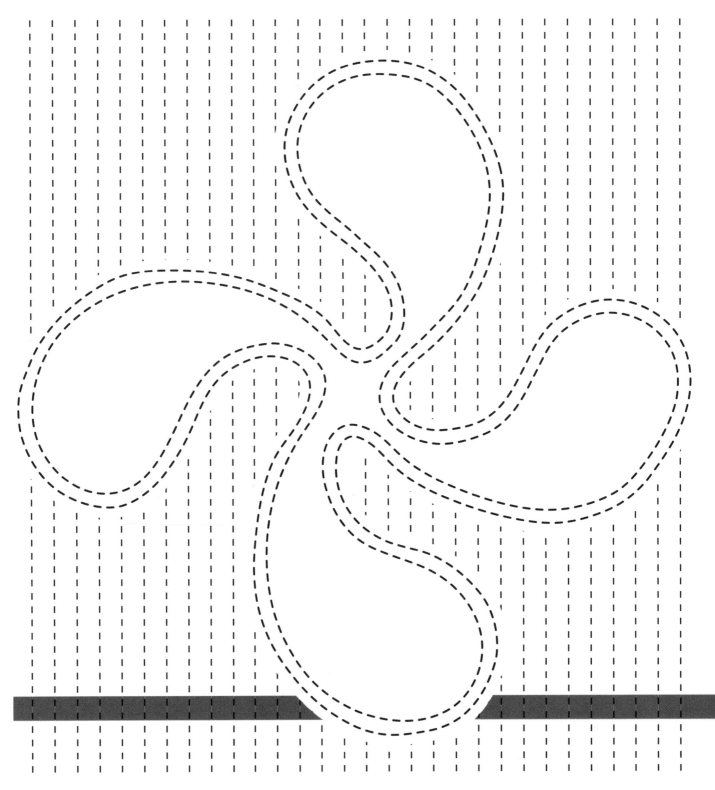

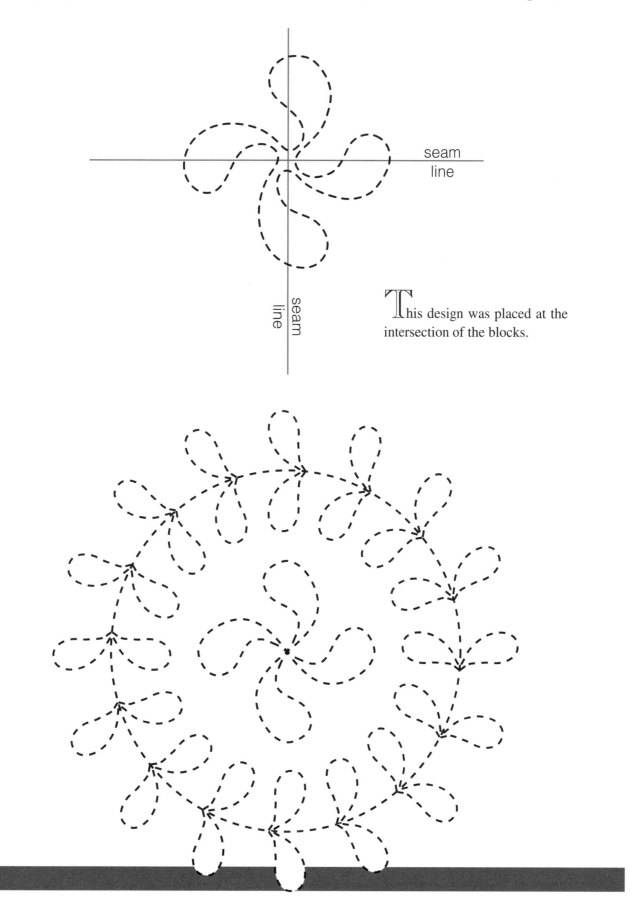

seam line

seam line

This design was placed at the intersection of the blocks.

Between the third and fourth rows, there
was a combination of miscellaneous motifs.

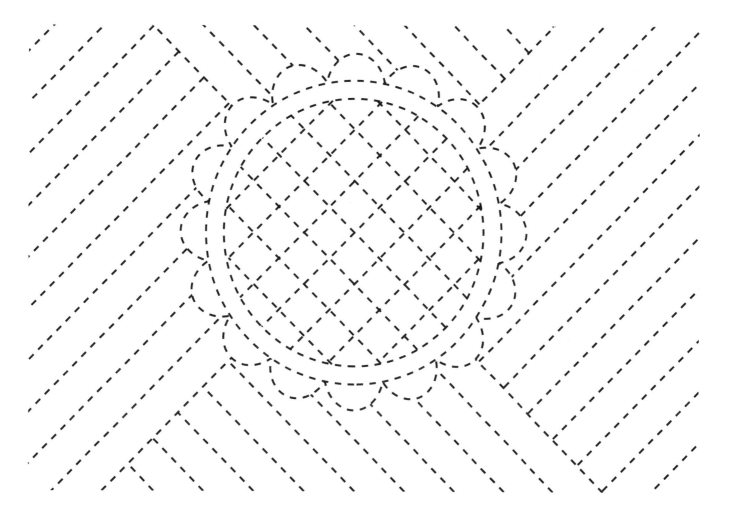

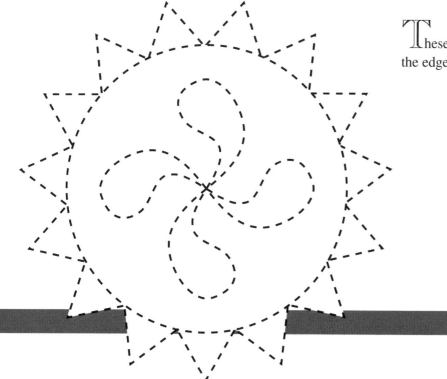

These two designs were alternated along the edge of the quilt next to the border.

PIECED DOUBLE IRISH CHAIN QUILT, circa 1845
Attributed to Mary Smith Maughlin, Airville, York County, Pennsylvania.
Collection of Lois A. Manifold.

When Mary Smith (b. 1797, d. 1867) and John Maughlin wed in 1817, they settled in Airville, York County, Pennsylvania. They raised 11 children, nine of whom survived to adulthood. A member of every succeeding generation, to this very day, has lived in the family's original house.

It is presumed that Mary Maughlin was the maker of this quilt. The Maughlins were Scots-Irish and members of the Presbyter-ian Church; however, the quilting designs show the influence of their German neighbors.

Once again, an Irish Chain has been chosen as a quilting sampler. The squares are arranged in a straight rather than diagonal setting. The first and third borders have been appliquéd to the central plain border strip. Since the fabrics are a solid red and green, dating is more difficult. Circa 1845 is a reasonable estimate. The stitches average 10 to the inch on this quilt.

This pattern resembles the Wheel of Fortune, a design that is seen most frequently on barn signs.

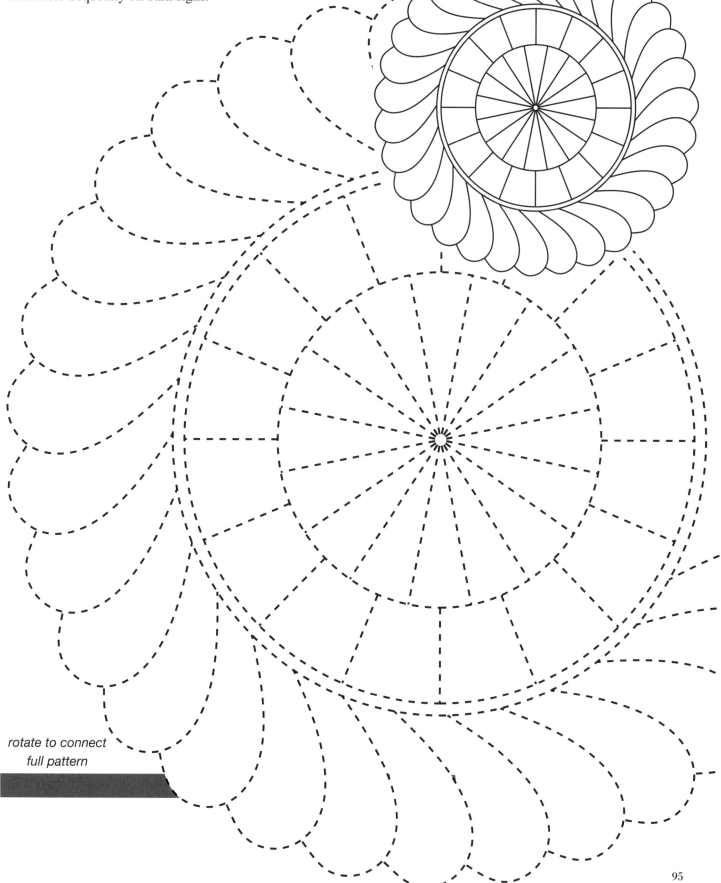

rotate to connect full pattern

*rotate to connect
full pattern*

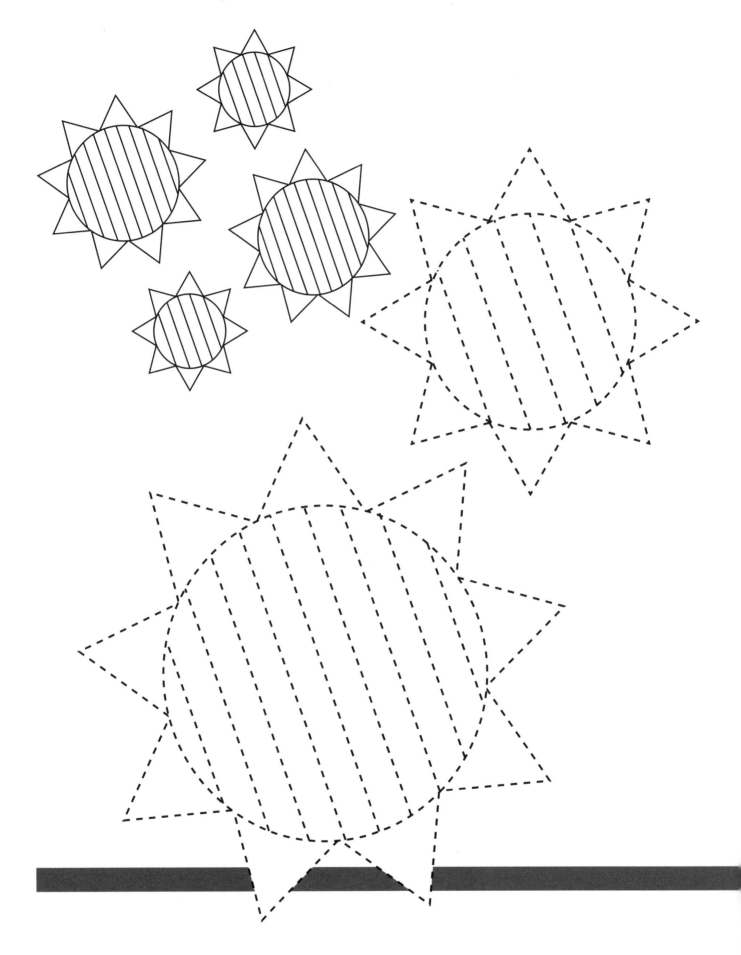

rotate to connect
full pattern

one quarter shown,
rotate to connect full pattern

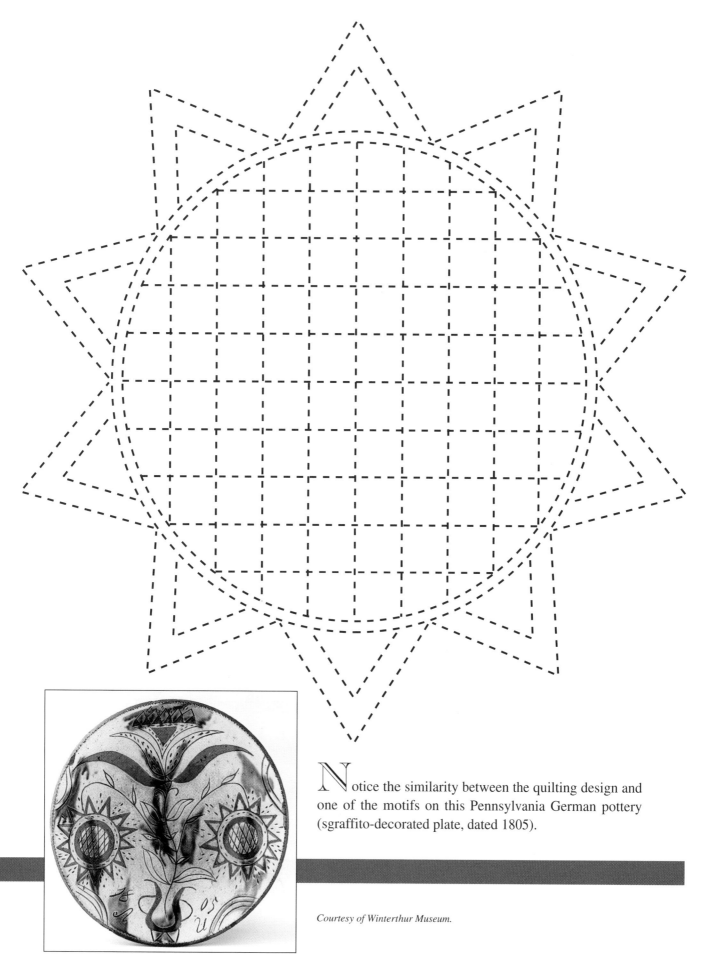

Notice the similarity between the quilting design and one of the motifs on this Pennsylvania German pottery (sgraffito-decorated plate, dated 1805).

Courtesy of Winterthur Museum.

placement diagram

connect here

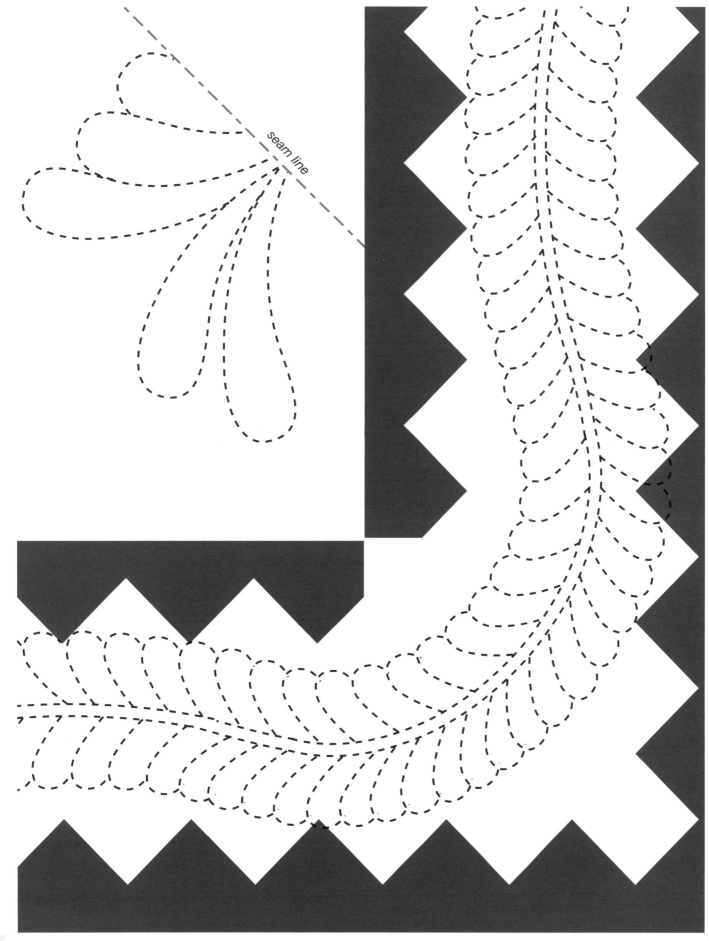

seam line

placement diagram

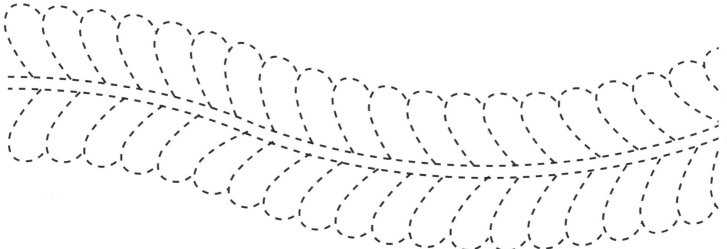

placement diagram

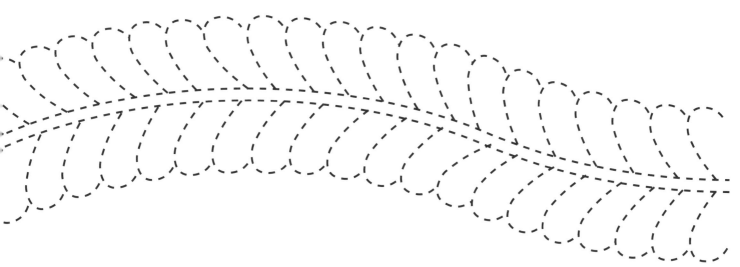

Recipes

Copied exactly as written in a Receipt (the old word for recipe) Book, dated 1832, from the collection of the author. It includes misspellings and punctuation marks, or lack thereof.

Indigo Blue – *Take 4 oz of Indigo, 4 oz of Madder, 1 of Alum, 8 of Potash to 10 gallons of water. Mix all well together and let it stand for two days when the dye is fit for use. This quantity is for 8 lb. of deep blue on Cotton or Linen, or 10 on Woolen.*

Turkey Red – *Take 2 oz Cochineal, 1 lb of Madder, 4 oz Alum, 1 lb of Red Sanders. Boil all in 10 gallons of water one hour. This quantity is for 8 lb of Turkey Red on Cotton or 10 lb of Scarlet on Woolens. Warranted not to fade.*

Pink – *To 2 lb of yarn take 5 oz of Alum, 1 oz Cochineal, and 1 oz Cream Tartar. Crimson, dye red with Brazil, when it becomes a good colour take it out let it get half dry then dip it in Lye.*

Yellow Wash – *Take ½ lb Chrome Yellow, ¾ lb best Whitning, 4 oz Gum arabic boiled in 3 qts water and mixed warm with the rest of the ingredients which should be well ground, first put on quick with a white wash brush very carefully, let it be the thickness of paint. The yellow has never failed when made after this Receipt.*

Nankin Dye – *Take a pail full of Lye with a piece of Copperas half as big as a hens egg boiled in it and it will produce a fine Nankin colour and will not wash out.*

For Colouring Scarlet – *Take 1½ oz Cream Tartar, infuse in warm water, for every pound of yarn, the bath is stirred and when the heat is increased add 1¼ oz Cochineal the whole to be mixed immediately afterwards, add 1¼ oz Solution of Tin stir it carefully, and when the bath begins to boil the yarn is put in and briskly moved two or three times, afterwards more slowly, let it boil 15 or 20 minutes then take it out and rinse it well.*

Orange – *To 3 lb of yarn, 2½ lb Fustic, 2 oz Cream Tartar, 2 oz Cochineal, 4 oz Solution of Tin, boil it thoroughly, after the Chips are skimmed out add the other ingredients, and treat it as the Scarlet – Solution of Indigo made by mixing 1 oz indigo with 4 oz Oil of Vitriol.*

About the Author

A beginning quilting class in an adult education program in 1984 initiated Roberta Benvin as a quilter. Four years later, she was elected president of the York Quilters Guild in Pennsylvania, and also began four years of employment in a quilt shop. Within a few months, Roberta was teaching classes at the shop and eventually took over the quilting classes for the adult education program. While working in the quilt shop, Roberta restored antique quilts in response to requests from customers. The restoration has since developed into a full-time business.

Roberta's passion for antique quilts has led to her involvement in the York County Quilt Documentation Project of Pennsylvania which gave Roberta the opportunity to examine numerous early nineteenth-century quilts.

Recent quilting projects of Roberta's have focused primarily on making reproductions of antique quilts, resulting in her awareness of a need for authentic quilting designs from the early 1800s.

Roberta has resided in York County, Pennsylvania, since 1969, and has three grown children.

Sources

In addition to the designs in this book, there is a line of stencils with additional patterns dating from the first half of the 1800s. The stencils may be ordered from your local quilt shop, favorite mail order catalog, or directly from the following:

Retail inquiries – The Stencil Company, 28 Castlewood Drive, Cheektowaga, NY 14227
Phone: 716-656-9430; website: www.quiltingstencils.com

Wholesale inquiries – Quilting Creations International, Inc., P.O. Box 512, Zoar, OH 44697
Phone: 877-219-9899 (toll free); fax: 330-874-3200; e-mail: qci@raex.com

Other AQS Books

This is only a small selection of the books available from the American Quilter's Society. AQS books are known worldwide for timely topics, clear writing, beautiful color photos, and accurate illustrations and patterns. The following books are available from your local bookseller, quilt shop, or the public library.

#6006   US $25.95

#5817 11" x 14"   US $16.95

#6009   US $19.95

#5235   US $18.95

#5928   US $16.95

#5894   US $29.95

#5177   US $15.95

#4827 5½" x 8½"   US $24.95

#4829 (HB)   US $24.95

Look for these books nationally or call 1-800-626-5420